ABSTRACT

The rapid advancement of technology and the evolving societal landscape have brought about a paradigm shift in the field of library science. Libraries, once considered bastions of print resources, are now transforming into dynamic information hubs that embrace the digital age. As libraries strive to remain relevant and effective in serving their communities, it becomes crucial to navigate the intricacies of the new library information science laws. This groundbreaking book, "Navigating the Digital Frontier: A Comprehensive Guide to New Library Information Science Laws and a Groundbreaking Proposal "serves as a compass for libraries worldwide as they adapt to the ever-changing technological landscape. Drawing upon the foundational principles of the traditional "five laws of library science" proposed by S.R. Ranganathan, this book sheds light on how these principles intertwine with the new laws, which are more attuned to the digital revolution and its impact on library services.

The book explores the pivotal role of technology in modern libraries, highlighting the essential tools required for successful implementation. It delves into the realm of Integrated Library Systems (ILS), Digital Content Management Systems, Library Discovery Tools, Open Access and Institutional Repositories, and Digital Preservation Systems. Through practical examples and case studies, readers gain insights into how these technologies empower libraries to provide seamless access to information, foster innovation, and build vibrant communities. This comprehensive guide illuminates the significance of digital literacy, showcasing a myriad of tools and resources that libraries can employ to enhance patrons' digital competencies. From online tutorials and workshops to computer labs and personalized assistance, the book offers a roadmap to develop essential digital skills and ensure equitable access to digital resources for all.

The book also explores emerging technologies, such as 3D printers, virtual reality, robotics, and maker spaces, which enable libraries to embrace innovation and provide patrons with hands-on experiences. It elucidates the transformative power of these technologies in fostering creativity, problem-solving, and collaboration, thereby positioning libraries as innovation hubs in their communities. The book addresses the critical aspect of digital security and privacy, showcasing a range of tools and practices to safeguard user data, protect network infrastructure, and promote responsible digital behavior. It underscores the importance of establishing secure connections, using encryption software, and implementing robust digital security measures in an increasingly interconnected world.In essence, "Navigating the Digital Frontier: A Comprehensive Guide to New Library Information Science Laws" equips library professionals, educators, policymakers, and researchers with the knowledge and strategies necessary to embrace the digital era fully. It serves as a roadmap for libraries worldwide, fostering their evolution into vibrant information centers that connect,

NAVIGATING THE DIGITAL FRONTIER: A COMPREHENSIVE GUIDE TO NEW LIBRARY INFORMATION SCIENCE LAWS AND A GROUNDBREAKING PROPOSAL

Dr. L. Radha
Librarian,
Thiagarajar College of Engineering, Madurai
radhalib@tce.edu
ORCID: 0000-0001-6959-5936

Dr. J. Arumugam
Librarian,
Dr.GRD Memorial Library
PSG College of Technology, Coimbatore
jam.lib@psgtech.ac.in
ORCID: 0000-0002-3349-8058

Dr. Mayank Trivedi
University Librarian,
The Maharaja Sayajirao University of Baroda
librarian-hml@msubaroda.ac.in
ORCID: 0000-0003-1834-5376

SHANLAX PUBLICATIONS

Title:	Navigating the Digital Frontier: A Comprehensive Guide to New Library Information Science Laws and a Groundbreaking Proposal
Author's Name:	Dr. L. Radha, Dr. J. Arumugam & Dr. Mayank Trivedi
Published by:	Shanlax Publications, Vasantha Nagar, Madurai – 625003, Tamil Nadu, India
Publisher's Address:	61, 66 T.P.K. Main Road, Vasantha Nagar, Madurai – 625003, Tamil Nadu, India
Printer's Details:	Shanlax Press, 66 T.P.K. Main Road, Vasantha Nagar, Madurai – 625003, Tamil Nadu, India
Edition Details (I,II,III):	I
ISBN:	978-81-19337-06-4
Month & Year:	July, 2023

Pages:	70
Price:	₹190/-

educate, innovate, and build thriving communities in the digital age.

Keywords: Navigating the Digital Frontier, Comprehensive Guide, New Laws of Library and Information Science, Laws of LIS, Laws for Library Science, Digital Age, Access to Information, Digital Preservation in Library Law, Five Laws of Library and Information Science, Groundbreaking Proposal of New Library Science Law

ACKNOWLEDGEMENT

I am immensely grateful for the invaluable assistance provided by Chat GPT and other AI tools throughout the journey of writing this book. Their remarkable capabilities and innovative algorithms have played an integral role in shaping and refining the content of this work.

I extend my heartfelt appreciation to the dedicated team of researchers, developers, and engineers who have tirelessly worked to create and improve these AI technologies. Your dedication to advancing the boundaries of human creativity and knowledge is truly commendable.

I would also like to express my thanks to the broader AI community for sharing insights, resources, and expertise that have enriched my understanding and application of these tools.

Furthermore, I am indebted to my readers, who will undoubtedly benefit from the collaboration between human ingenuity and artificial intelligence. Your curiosity and engagement drive me to explore new frontiers of writing and knowledge dissemination.

Finally, I acknowledge that while AI has played a significant role in the creation of this book, the ideas, interpretations, and personal touch infused into its pages are a reflection of my own thoughts and experiences.

Thank you, ChatGPT, other AI tools, and all those who have contributed to this endeavor. Your support has been instrumental, and I am excited to share the final product with the world.

INTRODUCTION

The field of library science has undergone a significant transformation in recent years, driven by the rapid advancement of technology and the changing needs of society. Libraries, once predominantly associated with physical spaces housing books, have evolved into dynamic information hubs that embrace the digital age. To navigate this new landscape effectively, libraries require a fresh perspective and a set of guiding principles that reflect the realities of the digital era.In this context, the concept of new library information science laws has emerged, emphasizing the need for libraries to adapt to new technologies and societal demands. While the traditional "five laws of library science" proposed by S.R. Ranganathan in the 1930s provided a solid foundation for library services, the new laws build upon these principles and incorporate the transformative impact of digital innovations. The new library information science laws recognize the crucial role of technology in shaping the modern library landscape. They encompass a range of aspects, including connectivity, inclusivity, learning, innovation, and community building. These laws acknowledge that libraries are no longer just repositories of knowledge, but rather vibrant centers that facilitate access to information, foster digital literacy, promote innovation, and strengthen community bonds.

With the advent of Integrated Library Systems (ILS), libraries can efficiently manage their collections, automate tasks, and provide seamless access to diverse resources.

Digital Content Management Systems allow libraries to curate and share digital content, expanding the range of materials available to patrons. Library Discovery Tools enhance information retrieval, enabling users to navigate vast digital collections with ease.The rise of Open Access and Institutional Repositories empowers libraries to promote knowledge sharing and scholarly communication.

Digital Preservation Systems ensure the long-term accessibility and integrity of digital materials, safeguarding valuable resources for future generations. Additionally, libraries harness the power of data analytics and usage statistics to better understand user needs and tailor their services accordingly.The new laws also underscore the importance of digital security and privacy in an increasingly interconnected world. Libraries must employ robust tools and practices to protect user data and educate patrons about safe online practices. Furthermore, collaboration and communication tools enable libraries to foster partnerships, engage with their communities, and maximize their impact.Embracing emerging technologies like maker spaces and incorporating digital literacy tools and resources helps libraries empower individuals and bridge the digital divide. By providing access to technology, skills training, and online resources, libraries can ensure that all members of society have the opportunity to thrive in the digital realm.

The new library information science laws reflect the changing landscape of libraries in the digital age. They highlight the importance of technology, connectivity, innovation, and community engagement in shaping the modern library. By adhering to these laws, libraries can adapt, evolve, and continue to serve as vital resources in an increasingly digital and interconnected world.

In an age where information and knowledge play a paramount role in shaping societies, it is imperative that our library information science laws evolve to meet the dynamic challenges of the digital era. The advent of technology, the internet, and the proliferation of digital content have reshaped the landscape of information consumption and distribution. This proposal seeks to enact groundbreaking legislation that addresses these challenges and transforms libraries into vibrant hubs of knowledge, accessibility, and innovation. This book covers the following topics since it's a ground breaking proposal.

Digital Accessibility and Inclusion

Recognizing the importance of equal access to information, this section emphasizes the need to make digital content and resources available to all, regardless of physical abilities or socio-economic status. Libraries must be required by law to ensure that their digital interfaces, catalogs, and resources are accessible through assistive technologies, and to provide training for their staff to support users with varying needs.

Open Access and Digital Preservation

In light of the digital age's impermanence, this section mandates libraries to champion open access initiatives and prioritize digital preservation efforts. Libraries should be mandated to collaborate with publishers, content creators, and archiving organizations to ensure that a diverse range of digital materials, including scholarly articles, cultural artifacts, and community-generated content, are preserved and made accessible for future generations.

Privacy and Ethical Data Management

In this era of data-driven decision-making, libraries must be at the forefront of safeguarding user privacy and promoting ethical data management. This section requires libraries to adopt stringent data protection practices, ensuring that user data is not exploited for commercial gains or surveillance purposes. Additionally, libraries should be empowered to educate their users about digital privacy rights and responsible data sharing.

Collaborative Innovation Hubs

Acknowledging the evolving role of libraries, this section envisions libraries as collaborative innovation hubs. Libraries should be empowered to partner with local educational institutions, technology companies, startups, and community organizations to foster creativity, entrepreneurship, and technological literacy. This may include providing spaces for co-working, hosting technology workshops, and facilitating maker spaces for hands-on learning.

Information Literacy and Digital Fluency

Given the deluge of information in the digital realm, libraries must take the lead in promoting information literacy and digital fluency. This section mandates libraries to develop comprehensive information literacy programs for users of all ages, teaching critical thinking, source evaluation, and responsible online behavior. These programs should adapt to the evolving information landscape and technological advancements.

Funding and Support

To enact these ambitious changes, adequate funding and support are crucial. This section proposes the allocation of a designated portion of government funding for library modernization, technological infrastructure upgrades, staff training, and community outreach efforts. Additionally, libraries should be encouraged to seek partnerships and grants to supplement their resources and expand their impact.

The world of information is rapidly evolving, driven by technological advancements, changes in user behaviors, and the proliferation of digital content. As custodians of knowledge, libraries must adapt to these changes and continue to serve as accessible and reliable sources of information for all individuals. This proposal outlines a series of innovative laws designed to address the evolving landscape of library and information science.

- To propose and advocate for the adoption and implementation of the new laws of library and information science in the LIS curriculum

- To establish a comprehensive set of new laws and regulations aimed at modernizing and optimizing library and information science practices, ensuring equitable access to information, fostering digital literacy, and supporting the evolving information landscape.
- To ensure equitable access to information for all individuals, regardless of socioeconomic status or geographical location.
- To enhance digital and information literacy skills among users to help them navigate the complex information landscape effectively.
- To protect users' privacy rights while upholding intellectual freedom and ensuring that libraries remain safe spaces for exploration and learning.
- To foster collaboration between libraries, information institutions, and technology stakeholders to drive innovation and adapt to emerging trends.
- To preserve cultural heritage by digitizing and archiving historical materials while ensuring their accessibility for future generations.

Some of the Specific objectives are

- To raise awareness and understanding of the new laws of library and information science among educators, policymakers, and stakeholders in the LIS field.
- To evaluate the current state of the LIS curriculum and identify areas that need to be updated or enhanced to align with the principles outlined in the new laws.

- To propose specific recommendations and guidelines for integrating the new laws into the LIS curriculum, including the incorporation of relevant courses, topics, and practical experiences.
- To explore the potential impact of adopting the new laws on the knowledge, skills, and competencies of future librarians and information professionals.
- To assess the challenges and opportunities associated with implementing the new laws in the LIS curriculum, considering factors such as available resources, faculty expertise, and technological infrastructure.
- To highlight the benefits and outcomes of incorporating the new laws in the LIS curriculum, such as improved preparedness of graduates, enhanced digital literacy skills, and the ability to meet the evolving needs of library users and communities.
- To provide a roadmap for educational institutions and policymakers to adopt and implement the new laws in the LIS curriculum, including strategies for faculty development, collaboration with industry professionals, and continuous evaluation and improvement.

In a rapidly changing information landscape, libraries must evolve to remain relevant and accessible to all members of society. This proposal aims to set the groundwork for modernizing library and information science practices, promoting equitable access to information, enhancing digital literacy, and safeguarding user privacy. By enacting these groundbreaking laws, we can ensure that libraries continue to serve as vital pillars of knowledge and learning in the digital age. The overall objective is to contribute to the advancement of library and information science education by promoting a forward-thinking approach that prepares future professionals to effectively navigate the digital era and fulfill the evolving roles and responsibilities of libraries in society.

Groundbreaking Proposal

In the current digital age, new laws of library science may be necessary to reflect the changing nature of libraries and the ways in which they serve their communities. New laws in library and information science are essential to adapt to the digital era, ensure equitable access to information, protect user rights, and guide libraries in their evolving roles. These laws can empower libraries to continue serving as vital institutions in promoting education, information literacy, and democratic principles.

Need of New Laws of Library Science

The need for new laws in library and information science arises from the rapidly evolving technological, societal, and informational landscape. Existing laws and regulations may not adequately address the challenges and opportunities that modern libraries face. Digital Transformation that shift towards digital content and online resources requires new legal frameworks to address issues related to digital access, preservation, privacy, and security. Traditional laws may not cover digital rights, licensing, and data management adequately.

Equitable Access in an increasingly digital world, ensuring information becomes crucial. New laws can address digital divides, mandate internet connectivity in libraries, and promote open access initiatives to provide everyone with fair access to knowledge.

Data Privacy and Security in libraries. Libraries collect and manage user data for various purposes. New laws can establish guidelines on data protection, consent, and cybersecurity to ensure that users' privacy rights are upheld and sensitive information is safeguarded.

Intellectual Freedom in the digital world where the internet age brings challenges to intellectual freedom, including issues of censorship, filtering, and the right to access diverse viewpoints. New laws can reinforce intellectual freedom principles while adapting to new forms of information dissemination.

Digital Literacy and Education in Libraries. With the proliferation of information online, digital literacy is crucial for individuals to critically evaluate and use information effectively. Laws can mandate the inclusion of digital literacy in educational curricula and require libraries to provide resources and training.

Copyright and Fair Use Policy in the digital environment. Digital content and sharing platforms have complicated copyright issues. New laws can address fair use, licensing, and digital rights management to balance creators' rights with users' access needs.

Libraries play a role in preserving cultural heritage. New laws can outline requirements for digitization, archiving, and accessibility of historical materials, considering copyright, digitization standards, and accessibility for diverse audiences.

Technological Innovation plays a vital role in libraries. As libraries adopt new technologies like AI, virtual reality, and big data, laws can guide responsible and ethical implementation, data governance, and the protection of user rights within these technologies.

New laws can encourage collaborations between libraries, governmental bodies, private enterprises, and educational institutions to harness collective resources and expertise for the benefit of society.

Adaptation to Emerging Trends is the way to accept the digital challenges. Traditional laws may not address emerging challenges such as fake news, deepfakes, and algorithmic bias. New laws can provide frameworks for addressing these issues within the library context.

Global Information Flow where Libraries are part of a global information network. New laws can facilitate international collaboration, information sharing, and adherence to international standards.

Libraries have expanded roles as community centers, learning hubs, and safe spaces. New laws can support these roles by addressing funding, community engagement, and programmatic mandates.

Proposed New Laws of Library Science

Libraries are for connection

Libraries are now centers of community and connection. They provide opportunities for users to connect with one another, build relationships, and engage in meaningful dialogue. By creating spaces for social interaction, libraries can foster a sense of community and help build strong, connected, and supportive communities. Additionally, libraries can provide access to technology and resources that facilitate digital connections and help users stay connected to one another and to the world at large.

Libraries for all

Libraries should strive to provide equal access to information and resources for all members of their communities, regardless of socio-economic status, race, gender, or other factors. This is a key principle of inclusive library services, and it is important for libraries to ensure that all members of their communities have equal access to information, resources, and opportunities. This may involve providing technology and digital resources, offering programming and events that serve diverse communities, and working to ensure that all members of the community feel welcome and included in the library. By promoting equity and inclusion, libraries can play a vital role in promoting social justice and building stronger, more inclusive communities.

Libraries are learning centers

Libraries are becoming increasingly important as centers of lifelong learning. They provide opportunities for users to expand their knowledge, skills, and abilities through access to information, resources, and programming. This can include traditional resources such as books, journals, and databases, as well as more modern resources such as online learning platforms, makerspaces, and virtual reality environments.

By embracing technology and innovation, libraries can create dynamic learning environments that engage users and help them develop new skills and knowledge. Furthermore, libraries can also provide support and resources for individuals who are seeking to upskill or reskill in order to stay current in a rapidly changing job market.

Libraries are innovation hubs

Libraries should be places where new ideas, technologies, and innovations can be explored and developed. They should provide opportunities for users to experiment, collaborate, and create. This can include providing access to cutting-edge technology and resources, such as 3D printers, virtual reality equipment, and maker spaces. Additionally, libraries can offer programs and events that foster innovation and creativity, such as hackathons, workshops, and incubation programs.

By fostering innovation and creativity, libraries can help their communities stay on the cutting edge of technology and develop new solutions to the challenges they face. Furthermore, libraries can also serve as important catalysts for economic development, helping to foster innovation and entrepreneurship within their communities.

Libraries are community builders

These new laws reflect the evolving role of libraries in today's digital age and the ways in which they can provide value to their communities. By embracing these new laws, libraries can remain relevant and effective in serving their communities and meeting the changing needs of their users.

Libraries play a crucial role in building strong, connected, and vibrant communities. They provide opportunities for members of the community to come together, share experiences, and engage in meaningful dialogue. This can include offering programs and events that bring people together, such as book clubs, storytimes, and community meetings. Additionally, libraries can provide spaces for social interaction, such as lounge areas, community rooms, and outdoor spaces.

By creating these spaces for social interaction, libraries can help build strong, supportive communities that are better equipped to address the challenges they face. Additionally, libraries can help to bridge divides and bring together diverse communities, promoting understanding and fostering a sense of inclusiveness.

Comprehensive Guide to the New Law of Library and Information Science

The field of Library and Information Science (LIS) is undergoing a transformative shift in response to technological advancements, changing user behaviors, and the growing importance of equitable access to information. To address these changes, a comprehensive set of new laws has been developed to guide the modernization of libraries and information services. This guide outlines the key aspects of these new laws and their implications for the LIS sector. The new laws in library science should enable libraries to embrace technological advancements, promote equitable access to information, nurture digital literacy, protect user privacy, foster innovation, and continue serving as essential community institutions in the digital age.

Digital Access and Copyright

With the increasing reliance on digital resources, libraries need laws that govern the acquisition, licensing, and lending of digital materials. These laws should also address issues related to copyright, fair use, and digital rights management, enabling libraries to provide equitable access to digital content while respecting intellectual property rights.

Privacy and Data Protection

As libraries embrace technology and collect user data for various purposes, laws must protect the privacy and confidentiality of library users. Legislation should establish guidelines for data collection, storage, and usage to ensure that libraries safeguard sensitive information and maintain user trust.

Digital Literacy and Information Literacy

New laws should emphasize the importance of digital literacy and information literacy education within libraries. These laws can support the development of programs and resources that teach users how to navigate the digital landscape effectively, evaluate information critically, and develop essential digital skills.

Open Access and Open Science

Given the increasing importance of open access and open science initiatives, laws can promote the dissemination of research and knowledge. These laws might encourage libraries to support open access publishing, open educational resources, and open data initiatives, facilitating the free flow of information and fostering collaboration.

Digital Preservation and Archiving

With the transition to digital resources, libraries face challenges in preserving and archiving digital content effectively. New laws should address the long-term preservation of digital materials, ensuring that valuable digital content is not lost and remains accessible for future generations.

Community Engagement and Innovation

Laws can support libraries as community hubs and centers for innovation. They can encourage partnerships between libraries and local organizations, funding opportunities for community programs and events, and the integration of maker spaces and technology labs within library spaces.

Funding and Resource Allocation

As libraries adapt to new technologies and expand their services, laws can help secure adequate funding and resource allocation for libraries. Legislation might address budgeting, grants, and partnerships to ensure libraries have the necessary resources to meet evolving needs.

Comparing the traditional "Five Laws of Library Science" with the new laws of Library Science:

Books are for use vs. Libraries are for connection

The traditional law emphasizes the importance of books as resources meant to be used by library patrons. The new law emphasizes the role of libraries as spaces for connecting people, fostering social interactions, and building a sense of community.

Every reader his/her book vs. Libraries for all

The traditional law promotes the idea that every reader should be able to find a book that suits their needs. The new law extends this concept to emphasize that libraries should be accessible and inclusive to all individuals, regardless of their background, abilities, or interests.

Every book its reader vs. Libraries are learning centers

The traditional law suggests that every book has its reader, highlighting the importance of matching readers with appropriate materials. The new law focuses on the library as a center for learning, providing resources, programs, and services that support educational and knowledge acquisition activities.

Save the time of the reader vs. Libraries are innovation hubs

The traditional law encourages libraries to efficiently serve their patrons and save their time. The new law highlights the library's role as an innovation hub, where individuals can explore new ideas, access technological tools, and engage in creative and entrepreneurial endeavors.

Library is a growing organism vs. Libraries are community builders

The traditional law views the library as a dynamic entity that evolves and grows over time. The new law emphasizes the library's function as a community builder, emphasizing its role in bringing people together, fostering social connections, and creating a sense of belonging.

The new laws of library science reflect a shift in focus from solely providing access to books and saving time to encompassing broader aspects such as community building, innovation, and inclusivity. These new laws recognize the changing societal and technological landscape, emphasizing the library's role as a hub for connection, learning, and creativity in the digital age.

Course Design for Library Science as Per the New Laws

Creating a comprehensive course for designing a groundbreaking proposal for new laws in library science involves a structured approach that covers key concepts, skills, and practical application.

Introduction to the role of Libraries

This module will provide an overview of the course and introduce students to the importance and role of libraries in today's society, including their role as centers of connection, learning, innovation, and community building. The following are a possible outline of the content for an "Introduction to the role of Libraries" course:

- Overview of the course
  - Introduction to the course objectives, structure, and assessment methods.
- The history of libraries
  - A brief overview of the evolution of libraries, from ancient civilizations to the present day, including key milestones and innovations.
- The purpose of libraries
  - An exploration of the fundamental reasons for the existence of libraries, including access to information, knowledge, and culture.

- The role of libraries in society
  - A discussion of the various roles that libraries play in society, including as centers of learning, sources of information, and community hubs.
- The changing face of libraries
  - An examination of the ways in which libraries are adapting to changing technology and social trends, including the integration of digital technologies and the provision of new services.
- The future of libraries
  - A discussion of the challenges and opportunities facing libraries in the future, including the changing nature of information and technology, and the evolving needs of society.
- The importance of libraries
  - A reflection on the ongoing importance of libraries, and the ways in which they serve as essential institutions for the preservation and dissemination of knowledge, culture, and information.

The course may also include case studies, guest lectures, and discussions to help students better understand the role of libraries in the world and in their communities.

Libraries for Connection

This module will explore the ways in which libraries can connect people to information, resources, and each other, including through digital technologies and community outreach programs. The possible outline of the content for a "Libraries for Connection" course

- Overview of the module:
  - Introduction to the module objectives, structure, and assessment methods.
- The role of libraries in connecting people to information
  - An examination of the ways in which libraries provide access to information and resources, including through print and digital collections, databases, and interlibrary loan services.
- Connecting people to each other
  - A discussion of the role of libraries in fostering community and social connection, including through programming, outreach, and community engagement initiatives.
- Connecting people to technology
  - An exploration of the role of libraries in providing access to technology, including computers, internet access, and training programs.
- Connecting people to their communities
  - A examination of the ways in which libraries can serve as community hubs, including through partnerships with local organizations, community events, and outreach programs.
- Innovations in library connectivity
  - A discussion of the latest developments and innovations in library connectivity, including virtual reality, augmented reality, and the Internet of Things.
- Case studies
  - An examination of real-world examples of libraries that have successfully used technology and innovative

programming to connect people to information, each other, and their communities.

The course may also include hands-on activities, group discussions, and field trips to local libraries to help students understand the practical applications of the concepts covered in the module.

Libraries for All

This module will examine the importance of libraries as inclusive spaces that serve all members of the community, regardless of their background, abilities, or interests. The possible outline of the content for a "Libraries for All" course:

- Overview of the module
  - Introduction to the module objectives, structure, and assessment methods.
- The importance of inclusivity in libraries
  - A discussion of the principles of inclusivity and the ways in which libraries can promote diversity, equity, and access for all members of the community.
- Accessibility and assistive technologies
  - An examination of the role of libraries in providing access to information and technology for individuals with disabilities, including through assistive technologies and accessibility features.
- Serving diverse populations
  - A discussion of the various ways in which libraries can serve diverse communities, including through

specialized collections, programming, and outreach initiatives.

- Literacy and lifelong learning
  - An exploration of the role of libraries in promoting literacy and lifelong learning, including through early childhood programs, adult education initiatives, and digital learning opportunities.

- Community engagement and outreach
  - A discussion of the ways in which libraries can engage with and serve underrepresented communities, including through outreach programs, community partnerships, and advocacy initiatives.
- Case studies
  - An examination of real-world examples of libraries that have successfully served diverse populations and promoted inclusivity and accessibility.

The course may also include hands-on activities, group discussions, and guest lectures from library professionals and experts in related fields to provide students with a deeper understanding of the practical applications of the concepts covered in the module.

Libraries as Innovations Hubs

- Overview of the module
  - Introduction to the module objectives, structure, and assessment methods.

- The concept of innovation
  - A discussion of the principles and practices of innovation, including the latest theories and best practices.
- Libraries and innovation
  - An examination of the role of libraries as innovation hubs, including through the provision of resources, technology, and community spaces for learning, experimentation, and collaboration.
- Entrepreneurship and innovation in libraries
  - A discussion of the ways in which libraries can support and promote entrepreneurship and innovation, including through incubator programs, maker spaces, and technology hubs.
- Building a culture of innovation
  - An exploration of the steps libraries can take to foster a culture of innovation, including through leadership, staff development, and community engagement initiatives.
- Case studies
  - An examination of real-world examples of libraries that have successfully integrated innovation and entrepreneurship into their operations and services.
- Future trends and opportunities
  - A discussion of emerging trends and new opportunities for libraries to continue to innovate and evolve, including through the integration of artificial intelligence, virtual and augmented reality, and the Internet of Things.

The course may also include hands-on activities, group projects, and guest lectures from library professionals and innovation experts to provide students with a deeper understanding of the practical applications of the concepts covered in the module.

Libraries as Community Builders

In the ever-changing landscape of information and technology, libraries have evolved from being mere repositories of books to becoming vibrant hubs that play a central role in building and nurturing communities. This module explores the concept of libraries as community builders, focusing on their multifaceted roles in fostering connection, facilitating learning, and driving social change. The possible outline of the content for a "Libraries as Community Builders".

- Overview of the module
  - Introduction to the module objectives, structure, and assessment methods.
- The role of libraries as community hubs
  - A discussion of the ways in which libraries can serve as community hubs, including through the provision of resources, services, and community spaces.
- Building strong community partnerships
  - An examination of the role of libraries in building strong partnerships with local organizations, including schools, government agencies, and community-based organizations.

- Engaging with the community
  - A discussion of the various ways in which libraries can engage with and serve their communities, including through programming, outreach, and community events.
- Fostering community engagement and participation
  - An exploration of the steps libraries can take to foster community engagement and participation, including through volunteer programs, advocacy initiatives, and community feedback mechanisms.
- Building inclusive communities
  - A discussion of the ways in which libraries can promote inclusivity and access for all members of the community, including through diversity and equity initiatives.
- Case studies
  - An examination of real-world examples of libraries that have successfully served as community builders, including through partnerships, programming, and community engagement initiatives.

The course may also include hands-on activities, group projects, and field trips to local libraries to provide students with a deeper understanding of the practical applications of the concepts covered in the module.

When designing a course in library science, it's important to consider the current laws and regulations related to libraries and information management. It is also important to keep in mind that laws and regulations related to libraries and information management can change over time, so it's essential to regularly review and update the course content to ensure that it remains relevant and accurate.

The specific laws that may impact the course design would depend on the jurisdiction in which the course is being offered, but some common areas that may need to be addressed include

- Copyright laws which discuss the principles of copyright and fair use, and their impact on libraries and the creation and dissemination of information.
- Data privacy laws in exploring the regulations related to protecting the personal information of library patrons, and the responsibilities of libraries in this regard.
- Freedom of information laws to discuss the rights of individuals to access government-held information, and the role of libraries in facilitating this access.
- Digital rights management to examine the technologies and practices used to manage and protect digital content, and the implications for libraries and patrons.
- Library management and administration to cover the practical aspects of running a library, including budgeting, personnel management, and collection development.
- Emerging technologies in libraries where discuss new technologies and their impact on libraries and information management, such as automation, artificial intelligence, and virtual reality.

Key Technical Skills Required for Adapting to the New Laws of Library and Information Science

Adapting to the new laws of library and information science requires librarians and information professionals to possess a range of technology skills to effectively implement digital initiatives, ensure data privacy, and enhance user experiences. Here are some key technology skills that are crucial for adapting to the new laws

Integrated Library Systems (ILS)

ILS platforms are essential for managing library operations, including cataloging, circulation, acquisitions, and patron management. Upgrading to modern ILS systems enables libraries to efficiently handle digital resources, implement user-friendly interfaces, and streamline workflows.Examples of Integrated Library Systems (ILS) that are commonly used in libraries include:

- ❖ Koha is an open-source ILS that provides a comprehensive suite of features for managing library operations. It offers modules for cataloging, circulation, acquisitions, and online public access catalogs (OPAC). Koha is highly customizable and widely used by libraries of various sizes and types.
- ❖ Symphony developed by SirsiDynix, is a robust ILS that supports automation and management of library workflows. It offers features such as cataloging, circulation, serials management, acquisitions, and integrated discovery services. Symphony is known for its

scalability and is utilized by many large libraries and consortia.

- Alma developed by Ex Libris, is a cloud-based ILS that provides end-to-end library management services. It offers features for acquisitions, cataloging, circulation, electronic resource management, and analytics. Alma emphasizes integration with other library systems and supports collaborative workflows.
- Evergreen is an open-source ILS designed for consortia and large library systems. It offers features for cataloging, circulation, acquisitions, and resource sharing. Evergreen focuses on scalability, flexibility, and interoperability, making it a popular choice for shared library systems.
- Sierra: Sierra, developed by Innovative Interfaces, is an ILS that combines traditional library management features with modern functionality. It offers modules for cataloging, circulation, acquisitions, electronic resource management, and reporting. Sierra is known for its user-friendly interface and robust integration capabilities.

These are just a few examples of Integrated Library Systems available in the market. Libraries can select an ILS based on their specific needs, budget, and infrastructure, considering factors such as scalability, customization options, integration capabilities, and ongoing support and maintenance.

Digital Content Management Systems

Libraries need robust digital content management systems to effectively acquire, organize, store, and provide access to digital resources such as e-books, e-journals, databases, and multimedia materials. These systems ensure efficient discovery and retrieval of digital content for library users.

Examples of Digital Content Management Systems (CMS) commonly used in libraries include:

- DSpace is an open-source CMS designed specifically for managing and preserving digital content, including research papers, datasets, multimedia files, and more. It provides features for submission, storage, indexing, and retrieval of digital assets. DSpace is widely adopted by academic and research libraries.
- CONTENTdm is a popular digital content management platform used by libraries, museums, and cultural heritage institutions. It enables the creation, organization, and delivery of digital collections in various formats, including images, documents, audio, and video. CONTENTdm offers customizable interfaces and facilitates metadata management.
- Islandora is an open-source CMS built on Drupal, a widely used content management framework. It provides tools for creating and managing digital repositories, including the ingestion, organization, and presentation of diverse digital assets. Islandora supports integration with other systems and offers flexibility in customization.
- Omeka is a user-friendly CMS designed for creating and publishing digital exhibits and collections. It caters to the

needs of smaller institutions and individual researchers. Omeka allows users to curate and showcase digital content with rich metadata, customizable themes, and exhibit-building tools.

- Preservica is a digital preservation platform that goes beyond content management and focuses on long-term preservation of digital assets. It helps libraries ensure the authenticity, integrity, and accessibility of their digital collections over time. Preservica supports various file formats, metadata standards, and preservation workflows.
- Fedora Commons is an open-source CMS specifically designed for managing and preserving digital content. It provides a flexible infrastructure for storing and organizing digital assets, including support for versioning, access control, and metadata management. Fedora Commons emphasizes interoperability and integration with other systems.

Library Discovery Tools

Implementing modern library discovery tools helps users navigate and explore the library's resources effectively. These tools provide intuitive search interfaces, personalized recommendations, and advanced filtering options, enhancing the user experience and promoting the discovery of relevant information.Examples for Library discovery tools:

- EBSCO Discovery Service (EDS) is a comprehensive discovery tool that allows users to search and access a wide range of library resources, including books, e-books, journals, databases, and multimedia content. It provides a unified search interface, personalized recommendations, and advanced filtering options. EDS is widely adopted by academic libraries.

- Primodeveloped by Ex Libris, is a discovery and delivery solution that enables users to explore a library's physical and digital collections. It offers a user-friendly interface, faceted search, relevance ranking, and integration with library systems for seamless access to resources. Primo is used by various types of libraries, including academic, public, and special libraries.
- Summondeveloped by ProQuest, is a web-scale discovery service that provides users with a single search interface to access a library's resources. It covers a wide range of content types, including books, articles, audiovisual materials, and more. Summon offers features such as relevancy ranking, faceted navigation, and customizable branding.
- WorldCat Discoverydeveloped by OCLC, is a global library catalog and discovery tool. It allows users to search across the holdings of thousands of libraries worldwide, providing access to a vast collection of resources. WorldCat Discovery offers features like relevancy ranking, citation export, and interlibrary loan integration.
- VuFind is an open-source discovery interface that offers customizable search and discovery features. It supports various library resources, including books, articles, e-books, and digital collections. VuFind allows libraries to tailor the interface to their specific needs and integrate with different library systems.

- LibrarySearch is a discovery tool developed by Innovative Interfaces that offers a modern search experience for library users. It provides access to a library's physical and digital collections, including books, e-books, journals, and multimedia materials. LibrarySearch offers intuitive search capabilities, faceted navigation, and personalized features.

These examples represent a range of library discovery tools available to libraries. Each tool offers different features, functionalities, and integration options, allowing libraries to provide users with efficient and effective access to their resources. The selection of a library discovery tool depends on factors such as the library's collection, user needs, technical requirements, and budget.

Open Access and Institutional Repositories

Libraries can leverage technology to establish and maintain open access repositories. These platforms facilitate the dissemination of scholarly research, the preservation of digital content, and the promotion of open science initiatives.Examples of Open Access and Institutional Repositories commonly used in libraries include:

- DSpacementioned earlier as a digital content management system, also includes features for establishing institutional repositories. It allows libraries to create open access repositories to store and provide access to research outputs, scholarly articles, theses, dissertations, and other scholarly works. DSpace offers customization options and supports metadata standards.

- EPrints is an open-source software for building institutional repositories. It enables libraries to create and manage repositories for scholarly and research materials. EPrints supports open access publishing and provides features for metadata management, document uploading, versioning, and search capabilities.
- Digital Commons developed by bepress, is a hosted institutional repository platform used by many academic and research libraries. It allows libraries to showcase and disseminate their institution's scholarly outputs, including articles, conference proceedings, theses, and more. Digital Commons offers customization options, analytics, and integration with other systems.
- Figshare is a web-based platform that supports the hosting and sharing of research outputs and data. It allows researchers and institutions to create open access repositories for various types of research outputs, including datasets, figures, posters, and media files. Figshare provides features for versioning, citation tracking, and collaboration.
- Zenodo is an open-access repository developed by CERN and operated by OpenAIRE. It offers a platform for researchers to deposit and share their research outputs, including datasets, publications, and software. Zenodo assigns persistent identifiers to deposited works and provides integration with other research platforms.

- InvenioRDM is an open-source research data management platform that supports the creation of institutional repositories for research data. It provides features for secure storage, metadata management, and sharing of research datasets. InvenioRDM emphasizes compliance with data management best practices and supports open access principles.

These examples showcase the diversity of tools and platforms available for libraries to establish open access and institutional repositories. Each platform offers its own set of features, user interfaces, and customization options. The selection of an open access and institutional repository platform depends on factors such as the institution's needs, technical requirements, scalability, and sustainability.

Digital Preservation Systems

To ensure the long-term accessibility and preservation of digital materials, libraries require digital preservation systems. These systems employ various strategies, including data backup, format migration, metadata management, and fixity checks, to safeguard digital assets from degradation or loss.Examples of Digital Preservation Systems commonly used in libraries include:

- Archivematica is an open-source digital preservation system that provides tools and workflows for the long-term preservation and management of digital materials. It supports the creation of preservation packages, normalization of file formats, metadata extraction, and storage in archival formats. Archivematica emphasizes adherence to digital preservation standards and best practices.

- Preservica is a digital preservation platform that offers comprehensive solutions for managing and preserving digital content over time. It provides features such as automated file ingests, format validation, metadata management, fixity checks, and storage in secure preservation formats. Preservica supports the creation of preservation plans and ensures the integrity and accessibility of digital assets.
- Rosetta, developed by Ex Libris, is a digital preservation system designed for libraries, archives, and museums. It offers tools for ingest, preservation planning, format conversion, metadata management, and access to digital collections. Rosetta focuses on the long-term storage and preservation of digital content while providing access to authorized users.
- LOCKSS (Lots of Copies Keep Stuff Safe) is an open-source digital preservation system that uses distributed networks to store and preserve digital content. It creates multiple copies of digital assets across participating nodes, ensuring redundancy and protection against data loss. LOCKSS emphasizes decentralized preservation and community collaboration.
- The Archivists' Toolkit, now incorporated into ArchivesSpace, is a software application that supports archival description and management. While primarily focused on archival processing, it includes features for managing digital materials and preservation metadata. It

helps institutions organize and preserve digital assets alongside their physical collections.

- Arkivum is a digital preservation and archiving solution that offers secure storage and long-term preservation services. It provides features for data ingest, format validation, metadata management, and audit trails. Arkivum emphasizes data integrity, authenticity, and compliance with regulatory requirements.

These examples highlight a range of digital preservation systems that assist libraries in ensuring the long-term accessibility and integrity of their digital collections. The selection of a digital preservation system depends on factors such as the institution's preservation needs, technical requirements, scalability, and long-term sustainability goals.

Data Analytics and Usage Statistics

Libraries can utilize data analytics tools to gain insights into user behavior, resource usage patterns, and trends. By analyzing usage statistics, libraries can make informed decisions regarding collection development, resource allocation, and user engagement strategies.Examples of tools and platforms for data analytics and usage statistics commonly used in libraries include:

- Google Analytics is a widely used web analytics tool that provides detailed insights into website traffic, user behavior, and interactions. Libraries can implement Google Analytics on their websites to track user visits, popular pages, referral sources, and other metrics. It offers customizable reports and dashboards to analyze and visualize the data.

- COUNTER (Counting Online Usage of Networked Electronic Resources) is a widely adopted industry standard for measuring usage statistics of electronic resources, such as e-books, e-journals, and databases. It provides a consistent framework for collecting and reporting usage data, enabling libraries to track resource usage, understand user behavior, and make informed collection management decisions.
- LibInsight is a data analytics and visualization platform designed specifically for libraries. It offers tools for collecting, analyzing, and reporting library data, including circulation statistics, reference interactions, program attendance, and more. LibInsight helps libraries track key performance indicators, evaluate services, and demonstrate impact.
- Tableau is a powerful data visualization and analytics tool that enables libraries to explore, analyze, and present data in interactive and visually appealing ways. It supports connecting to various data sources, creating custom dashboards, and generating insights from complex datasets. Tableau helps libraries uncover patterns, trends, and correlations in their data.
- OpenRefine, formerly known as Google Refine, is an open-source data cleaning and transformation tool. It can be used by libraries to clean and standardize data, enhance metadata, and perform data analysis tasks. OpenRefine

offers features for data parsing, faceting, clustering, and reconciliation with external data sources.

- Alma Analytics is a module within the Alma library management system that provides built-in analytics and reporting capabilities. It enables libraries to generate custom reports, analyze circulation patterns, track resource usage, and assess collection performance. Alma Analytics offers a user-friendly interface and supports data visualization options.

These examples represent a variety of tools and platforms that libraries can use for data analytics and usage statistics. Each tool has its own features, capabilities, and data visualization options. The choice of a data analytics tool depends on factors such as the library's specific needs, data sources, technical expertise, and budgetary considerations.

Digital Security and Privacy Tools

With the increasing reliance on digital resources and user data, libraries need robust security measures to protect against cybersecurity threats and ensure user privacy. Implementing firewalls, encryption protocols, secure authentication systems, and data protection practices are crucial for safeguarding library systems and user information.Examples of digital security and privacy tools commonly used in libraries include:

- Virtual Private Network (VPN) creates a secure and encrypted connection between a user's device and the internet. It helps protect user privacy by masking their IP address and encrypting their online activities. Libraries can provide access to VPN services to ensure secure browsing and protect user data, especially when accessing library resources remotely.

- Secure Socket Layer (SSL) Certificates enable secure communication between a website and a user's browser. They encrypt data transmitted between the user and the website, preventing unauthorized access and ensuring data integrity. Libraries can implement SSL certificates on their websites to safeguard user data during online interactions.
- Password managers are tools that help users generate strong, unique passwords for different online accounts and securely store them. They encrypt passwords and provide convenient access to them when needed. Libraries can recommend password managers to users for secure password management and encourage good security practices.
- Firewalls are network security tools that monitor and control incoming and outgoing network traffic. They act as a barrier between internal networks and external networks, filtering out potential threats and unauthorized access attempts. Libraries can implement firewalls to protect their network infrastructure and prevent unauthorized access to sensitive data.
- Encryption software is used to encode data, making it unreadable to unauthorized individuals. It provides an extra layer of security for sensitive information, such as patron records or research data. Libraries can employ

encryption software to protect data at rest or during transmission, ensuring confidentiality and data integrity.

- Web Application Firewalls (WAF) are designed to protect web applications from common web-based attacks, such as cross-site scripting (XSS) or SQL injection. They analyze incoming web traffic, detect and block malicious requests, and safeguard web applications from vulnerabilities. Libraries can implement WAFs to protect their online platforms and user data.
- Two-Factor Authentication (2FA) adds an extra layer of security to user accounts by requiring users to provide an additional authentication factor, typically a unique code or fingerprint, in addition to their password. Libraries can encourage users to enable 2FA on their accounts to mitigate the risk of unauthorized access.

These examples demonstrate a range of digital security and privacy tools that libraries can employ to protect user data, secure their network infrastructure, and promote safe online practices. The selection of specific tools depends on the library's security requirements, available resources, and the level of protection desired.

Collaboration and Communication Tools

Libraries can leverage collaboration and communication technologies to foster partnerships, engage with the community, and facilitate knowledge sharing. These tools can include video conferencing platforms, project management systems, and online collaboration spaces.Examples of collaboration and communication tools commonly used in libraries include:

- Slack is a popular team communication platform that enables real-time messaging, file sharing, and collaboration. Libraries can create different channels for specific projects or teams, facilitating communication, document sharing, and discussions among staff members. Slack also integrates with various other tools and services to streamline workflows.
- Microsoft Teams is a collaborative platform that combines chat, video meetings, file sharing, and integration with Microsoft Office applications. Libraries can use Teams to facilitate communication and collaboration among staff members, organize virtual meetings, and work together on shared documents in real-time.
- Google Workspace (formerly G Suite) offers a suite of collaborative tools, including Gmail, Google Drive, Google Docs, Google Sheets, and Google Meet. Libraries can utilize these tools to foster collaboration and communication among staff members, allowing them to work on documents simultaneously, share files, and hold virtual meetings.
- Trello is a project management and collaboration tool that uses boards, lists, and cards to organize tasks and workflows. Libraries can create Trello boards to track projects, assign tasks to team members, and monitor progress. Trello provides a visual and intuitive interface to streamline collaboration and task management.

- Zoom is a video conferencing and collaboration platform that enables virtual meetings, webinars, and screen sharing. Libraries can use Zoom to facilitate remote communication and collaboration among staff members, host virtual events, and conduct online training sessions.
- Miro is an online collaborative whiteboarding platform that allows teams to ideate, brainstorm, and work together visually. Libraries can use Miro to facilitate collaborative planning, create visual workflows, and share ideas in a virtual environment.
- JIRA is a project management and issue tracking tool that helps teams manage tasks, track progress, and prioritize work. Libraries can use JIRA to organize and monitor projects, assign tasks to team members, and track issues or bugs in software development or other projects.
- GitHub is a web-based platform for version control and collaboration, primarily used in software development. Libraries can utilize GitHub to host and collaborate on open-source projects, track changes, and facilitate collaborative coding and development.

These examples represent a variety of collaboration and communication tools that libraries can employ to enhance teamwork, streamline workflows, and facilitate remote collaboration. The choice of specific tools depends on factors such as the library's collaboration needs, budget, technical infrastructure, and the preferences of the staff members.

Maker Spaces and Emerging Technologies

Libraries embracing the role of innovation hubs may incorporate emerging technologies such as 3D printers, virtual reality (VR) setups, robotics, and coding tools. These technologies foster creativity, experimentation, and learning, enabling users to engage in hands-on activities and explore new skills.Examples of maker spaces and emerging technologies commonly found in libraries include:

- 3D printers allow users to create three-dimensional objects by layering materials based on digital designs. Libraries with maker spaces often provide access to 3D printers, enabling patrons to bring their digital designs to life and explore the possibilities of additive manufacturing.
- Laser cutters use focused laser beams to cut or engrave materials such as wood, acrylic, or fabric. Libraries equipped with laser cutters provide users with the opportunity to create precise and intricate designs for various applications, including signage, prototypes, and artistic creations.
- Virtual Reality (VR) and Augmented Reality (AR) technologies immerse users in virtual or augmented environments, enhancing their sensory experiences. Libraries may offer VR and AR equipment and software, allowing patrons to explore virtual worlds, engage in educational experiences, or experiment with new forms of storytelling.
- Robotics and Electronics KitsforLibraries with maker spaces often provide robotics and electronics kits that allow users to experiment with building and

programming robots or electronic circuits. These kits foster hands-on learning, creativity, and problem-solving skills in areas such as coding, engineering, and circuitry.

- Internet of Things (IoT) Devices are everyday objects embedded with sensors, software, and connectivity, enabling them to collect and exchange data. Libraries may offer IoT devices for experimentation, allowing patrons to learn about smart home automation, environmental monitoring, or other IoT applications.
- Digital Media Production Tools for Libraries equipped with maker spaces often provide digital media production tools such as audio recording equipment, video cameras, green screens, and editing software. These tools empower patrons to create podcasts, videos, and other multimedia content, fostering digital storytelling and media literacy skills.
- Virtual learning platforms combine online educational content with interactive tools, quizzes, and assessments. Libraries may offer access to virtual learning platforms that provide self-paced courses on various subjects, empowering patrons to enhance their knowledge and skills in a flexible learning environment.
- Coding and Programming Resources for Libraries can offer coding and programming resources, including books, online tutorials, and coding platforms, to support patrons interested in learning programming languages and developing computer science skills.
- Emerging Technologies Exploration in Libraries can create spaces for patrons to explore and experiment with

emerging technologies that are still in development or gaining traction. This may include technologies like artificial intelligence, blockchain, wearable devices, or drone technology.

These examples illustrate some of the maker spaces and emerging technologies that libraries may incorporate to foster hands-on learning, creativity, and exploration among their patrons. The specific offerings may vary depending on the library's resources, community interests, and the ever-evolving landscape of emerging technologies.

Digital Literacy Tools and Resources

To support digital literacy initiatives, libraries can provide access to online tutorials, interactive learning platforms, and digital skills training resources. These tools empower users to navigate the digital landscape effectively, critically evaluate information, and utilize technology for personal and professional development.Examples of digital literacy tools and resources commonly used in libraries include:

- Online Tutorials and Courses in Libraries can provide access to online tutorials and courses that cover various digital literacy topics, such as computer basics, internet navigation, online safety, and digital skills development. Platforms like LinkedIn Learning, Coursera, or Khan Academy offer a wide range of digital literacy courses that patrons can access for free or at a reduced cost through library subscriptions.

- Digital Skills Workshops in Libraries can organize and host workshops or training sessions on specific digital skills, such as using productivity software (e.g., Microsoft Office, Google Workspace), social media platforms, online research techniques, or coding basics. These hands-on workshops allow patrons to gain practical experience and improve their digital competencies.
- Computer Labs in Libraries equipped with computer labs provide patrons with access to computers, internet connectivity, and software applications. Computer labs offer opportunities for individuals to develop and practice their digital literacy skills, explore online resources, and engage in activities like job searching, online learning, or creating digital content.
- One-on-One Assistance in Libraries can offer personalized assistance and guidance to patrons who need help with digital literacy. Trained staff members can provide one-on-one sessions to address specific digital literacy needs, answer questions, and offer support in navigating digital tools and resources.
- Online Safety and Privacy Resources in Libraries can curate resources and provide guidance on online safety, privacy, and security. This may include providing information on safe internet browsing, protecting personal information, avoiding online scams, and understanding privacy settings on social media platforms.
- Digital Literacy Assessment Tools in Libraries may use digital literacy assessment tools to evaluate patrons' existing skills and identify areas for improvement. These

tools can help libraries tailor their digital literacy programs and resources to better meet the needs of their patrons.

- E-book and Audiobook Platforms in Libraries can offer access to e-book and audiobook platforms, such as OverDrive or Libby, which allow patrons to borrow and read digital books or listen to audiobooks. Using these platforms promotes digital reading skills and familiarity with e-book technologies.
- Online Research Databases in Libraries provide access to online research databases and resources, such as academic journals, encyclopedias, and specialized databases. These resources help patrons develop information literacy skills, including effective search strategies, critical evaluation of sources, and proper citation practices.
- Digital Citizenship Resources in Libraries can offer resources and workshops focused on digital citizenship, including topics like online etiquette, responsible social media use, digital footprints, and ethical considerations in the digital world. These resources aim to cultivate responsible and ethical digital behavior among patrons.
- Technology Training Manuals and Guides in Libraries can develop or curate technology training manuals and guides that provide step-by-step instructions on using digital tools, software applications, or online platforms. These resources can be made available in print or digital formats for patrons to reference and learn at their own pace.

These examples highlight various tools and resources that libraries can provide to promote digital literacy skills among their patrons. The selection of specific tools and resources depends on the library's resources, community needs, and the desired outcomes for digital literacy initiatives.

Leveraging of Technology Alignment with New Laws of Library Science

Leveraging technology in alignment with the new laws of library and information science is essential to enhance library services, promote equitable access, ensure user privacy, and foster community engagement. By leveraging these technologies, libraries can effectively navigate and implement the new laws of library science, supporting their evolution as modern information centers in the digital age.

The new five laws of library science can be applied in libraries to guide their operations, services, and strategies. Here's how each of the new laws can be implemented:

Libraries are for Connection

- Libraries can prioritize creating connections among users, resources, and communities. This can be achieved by offering collaborative spaces, organizing community events, facilitating networking opportunities, and promoting digital connectivity.
- Libraries can also leverage technology to enhance online interactions, provide virtual services, and foster global connections.

Libraries for All

Libraries should strive to be inclusive and accessible to all individuals, regardless of their background, abilities, or socioeconomic status. This can be accomplished by offering diverse resources in multiple formats, ensuring physical and digital accessibility, providing language support, and tailoring services to meet the specific needs of different user groups.

Libraries are Learning Centers

Libraries can position themselves as lifelong learning hubs by offering a range of educational opportunities. This can include providing access to educational materials, organizing workshops, hosting guest speakers, facilitating skill development programs, and supporting digital literacy initiatives. Libraries can also embrace emerging technologies and promote continuous learning and professional development for staff.

Libraries are Innovation Hubs

Libraries can foster innovation by encouraging creativity, experimentation, and the exploration of new ideas. They can offer resources and support for entrepreneurship, technology incubation, and maker spaces. Libraries can also collaborate with local startups, innovators, and educational institutions to promote innovation and contribute to the growth of the local community.

- ❖ Libraries are Community Builders
- ❖ Libraries can actively engage with their communities and play a vital role in community development. They can

organize cultural events, facilitate discussions on important topics, support local initiatives, and provide spaces for community gatherings.

- Libraries can partner with community organizations, schools, and local authorities to address social issues, promote civic engagement, and enhance community well-being.

By applying these new laws, libraries can adapt to the changing needs of their users, leverage technology to expand their services, foster a sense of belonging and inclusivity, and serve as catalysts for learning, innovation, and community building. These laws provide a modern framework for libraries to remain relevant, dynamic, and integral in the digital age.

Application of New Laws in Indian Context

Libraries in India, like libraries worldwide, are facing the challenges and opportunities presented by the digital revolution. The growth of the internet, the availability of digital information, and the increasing emphasis on digital literacy and technology integration in education align with the core principles of the new library laws. These laws underscore the importance of connection, inclusivity, learning, innovation, and community building, which are essential for libraries to remain relevant and effective in serving their diverse user base.

In India, where access to digital resources and technology infrastructure may vary across regions, the application of these laws may require tailored approaches. Libraries can focus on bridging the digital divide by providing access to computers, internet connectivity, and digital tools in areas where they are lacking. They can collaborate with government initiatives, educational institutions, and community organizations to expand digital literacy programs and ensure that all segments of society can benefit from the digital resources and services offered by libraries.

Additionally, libraries in India can explore partnerships with content providers, publishers, and institutions to enhance digital content management, expand access to open educational resources, and develop institutional repositories. They can leverage library discovery tools to facilitate efficient information retrieval and offer personalized services to users. Libraries can also establish collaborations with local businesses, startups, and entrepreneurs to foster innovation and create spaces for emerging technologies, such as maker spaces, where patrons can experiment, create, and learn.

Addressing digital security and privacy concerns is crucial in the Indian context, given the increasing reliance on digital platforms and the need to protect user data. Libraries can prioritize implementing digital security measures, educating users about safe online practices, and advocating for policies that safeguard privacy rights.While the practical implementation of the new laws may vary depending on the resources and capacities of individual libraries, the overarching principles of adapting to new technologies, promoting digital literacy, fostering innovation, and building community connections can guide libraries in India towards transforming and remaining relevant in the digital era.

Pros of the New Laws of Library Science

The new laws of library science offer numerous benefits in terms of relevance, inclusivity, and community engagement, they also present challenges that need to be addressed for successful implementation. By proactively addressing these challenges, libraries can maximize the potential of the new laws and continue to play a vital role in serving their communities.

Relevance in the Digital Age

The new laws acknowledge the changing technological landscape and the need for libraries to adapt. They emphasize the importance of connectivity, digital literacy, and innovation, allowing libraries to remain relevant and meet the evolving needs of users.

Inclusivity and Accessibility

The focus on inclusivity and accessibility ensures that libraries cater to diverse user groups, including individuals with disabilities, different backgrounds, and varying levels of digital literacy. This promotes equal access to information and services, fostering a more inclusive society.

Lifelong Learning and Skill Development

The new laws recognize libraries as learning centers that provide educational opportunities beyond traditional book lending. They encourage continuous learning, skill development, and the acquisition of digital literacy skills, empowering individuals to thrive in the knowledge economy.

Innovation and Entrepreneurship

Libraries serving as innovation hubs can foster creativity, entrepreneurship, and the exploration of new ideas. By providing resources and support for innovation, libraries contribute to local economic development and encourage community members to engage in entrepreneurial activities.

Community Engagement and Social Impact

The emphasis on community building strengthens the relationship between libraries and their communities. Libraries can serve as gathering places, facilitate dialogue on important issues, and support local initiatives, contributing to social cohesion and positive social change.

Cons of the New Laws of Library Science

Resource Constraints

Implementing the new laws may require additional resources, both in terms of technology infrastructure and staffing. Libraries with limited budgets and staffing may face challenges in fully realizing the potential of the new laws and providing the desired level of services and support.

Digital Divide

While the new laws aim to promote digital literacy and connectivity, there may be challenges in ensuring equitable access to technology and addressing the digital divide. Libraries may need to develop strategies to reach marginalized communities and provide necessary support to bridge the digital gap.

Resistance to Change

Introducing new laws and transforming library practices may face resistance from traditionalists or individuals who are reluctant to embrace technological advancements. Overcoming resistance and fostering a culture of innovation and openness to change may require time, effort, and effective communication strategies.

Evolving Technological Landscape

The rapid pace of technological advancements means that libraries need to continuously adapt and upgrade their technology infrastructure to keep up with user expectations. This can pose challenges in terms of financial sustainability, technical expertise, and the need for ongoing training and professional development.

Balancing Traditional and Modern Roles

Libraries must strike a balance between preserving traditional library values, such as book lending and physical spaces, while embracing the new laws and evolving with digital technologies. This requires careful planning and effective management to ensure a harmonious integration of traditional and modern library practices.

Framework and Guidelines for Policy Changes

By developing and implementing a comprehensive policy, library systems can provide a clear roadmap for the adoption and integration of the new laws of library science. The policy serves as a guiding document that supports libraries in effectively implementing the laws, promoting consistency, and ensuring that the intended objectives are achieved.

Define the Policy Objective

Clearly articulate the objective of the policy, which is to implement the new laws of library science. This objective should align with the goals and vision of the library system.

Conduct Research and Analysis

Conduct a thorough research and analysis of the new laws, considering their implications, requirements, and potential impact on library operations. Identify specific areas where policy guidelines are needed to support the implementation of each law.

Engage Stakeholders

Consult and involve key stakeholders such as library staff, administrators, users, and relevant community members in the policy development process. Seek their input, feedback, and perspectives to ensure that the policy reflects the needs and expectations of all stakeholders.

Establish Policy Guidelines

Develop specific guidelines that outline how each law will be implemented within the library system. These guidelines should be practical, actionable, and measurable, providing clear directions for library staff to follow.

Consider Resource Allocation

Assess the resources required for effective implementation of the new laws and identify potential resource gaps. Determine how resources, including financial, technological, and human resources, will be allocated to support the implementation of the policy.

Training and Professional Development

Develop a plan for training and professional development programs to equip library staff with the necessary knowledge and skills to implement the new laws. Identify training needs, provide relevant workshops or courses, and encourage ongoing learning to keep staff updated with emerging trends and technologies.

Monitoring and Evaluation

Establish mechanisms for monitoring the implementation of the policy and evaluating its effectiveness. This can involve regular assessments, surveys, feedback mechanisms, and data analysis to measure the impact of the new laws on library services, user satisfaction, and community engagement.

Communication and Promotion

Develop a communication strategy to promote the new policy and raise awareness among library staff, users, and the wider community. Utilize various channels such as newsletters, websites, social media, and community events to disseminate information about the new laws and their implementation.

Review and Revision

Regularly review and revise the policy as needed to ensure its continued relevance and alignment with evolving technologies, societal needs, and best practices in the library field. Solicit feedback from stakeholders and incorporate their suggestions to improve the policy over time.

Define Policy to Implement the New Laws of Library and Information Science

This policy establishes guidelines and procedures for the implementation of the new laws of library and information science within our library system. It aims to ensure that the libraries under our jurisdiction effectively adapt to the changing technological and societal landscape, promote inclusivity, foster innovation, and provide valuable services to our communities.

Policy Objectives

- To align library practices with the new laws of library and information science, embracing the principles of connection, inclusivity, learning, innovation, and community building.

- To provide a framework for consistent and effective implementation of the new laws across all libraries within our system.
- To enhance access to information, promote digital literacy, and meet the diverse needs of library users.
- To foster a culture of innovation, collaboration, and lifelong learning among library staff.
- To strengthen community engagement, encourage civic participation, and contribute to the social well-being of our communities.

Policy Guidelines

- Connection
  - Establish and maintain a robust integrated library system (ILS) to facilitate seamless access to resources and services.
  - Promote digital connectivity by providing reliable and high-speed internet access in libraries and encouraging the use of digital tools for communication and collaboration.
- Inclusivity
  - Ensure physical and digital accessibility of library facilities, resources, and services for individuals with disabilities.
  - Develop collection policies that reflect the diversity of user needs, including materials in different languages, formats, and topics.

- Provide training and support for staff to interact sensitively with users from diverse backgrounds and communities.

- Learning
  - Offer a range of educational opportunities, including workshops, training programs, and information literacy sessions, to promote lifelong learning and skill development.
  - Collaborate with educational institutions to provide resources and support for formal and informal learning initiatives.
  - Foster a culture of continuous learning among library staff through professional development programs.
- Innovation
  - Create spaces and resources for innovation, such as maker spaces and emerging technology labs, to encourage creativity, experimentation, and entrepreneurship.
  - Promote the use of emerging technologies and digital content management systems to support innovative services and programs.
  - Establish partnerships with local startups, innovators, and organizations to foster innovation and contribute to the local ecosystem.
- Community Building
  - Organize cultural events, discussions, and community outreach programs to facilitate community engagement and address local needs.

- Collaborate with community organizations, schools, and local authorities to address social issues and promote civic participation.
- Provide meeting spaces and resources for community groups and initiatives that align with the library's mission and values.

Policy Implementation

- Responsibility
  - The library administration is responsible for ensuring the implementation of this policy.
  - Library staff members are responsible for familiarizing themselves with the policy guidelines and incorporating them into their daily practices.
- Training and Communication
  - Conduct regular training sessions to educate library staff about the new laws and their implications.
  - Communicate the policy guidelines to library staff, users, and other stakeholders through various channels, such as staff meetings, newsletters, and the library website.
- Monitoring and Evaluation
  - Regularly monitor the implementation of the policy through performance assessments, user feedback, and data analysis.
  - Evaluate the effectiveness of the policy in achieving its objectives and make necessary adjustments based on the findings.

- Policy Review
  - Review the policy periodically, considering emerging trends, technological advancements, and user feedback.
  - Revise the policy as needed to ensure its continued relevance and effectiveness in supporting the libraries within our system.

Conclusion

New laws of library science, which emphasize the adaptation of libraries to the digital age and evolving societal needs, hold practical applicability for libraries in India. These laws recognize the changing role of libraries as information hubs and highlight the importance of connection, inclusivity, learning, innovation, and community building. Implementing new laws in library science can bring about significant changes in how library science courses are designed and delivered. These changes will reflect the evolving role of libraries in the digital age, focusing on equitable access, digital literacy, privacy protection, and community engagement.

For libraries in India, implementing the new laws requires tailored approaches that address the specific challenges and opportunities within the local context. Bridging the digital divide and ensuring equitable access to digital resources and technology infrastructure are key considerations. Libraries can collaborate with government initiatives, educational institutions, and community organizations to expand digital literacy programs and provide access to computers, internet connectivity, and digital tools.Furthermore, libraries in India can leverage partnerships with content providers, publishers, and institutions to enhance digital content management and expand access to open educational resources. They can adopt library discovery tools to improve information retrieval and offer personalized services to users. Collaborations with local businesses, startups, and entrepreneurs can foster innovation and create spaces for emerging technologies like maker spaces.

Addressing digital security and privacy concerns is paramount in the Indian context, given the increasing reliance on digital platforms. Libraries can prioritize the implementation of digital security measures, educate users on safe online practices, and advocate for privacy protection policies.By embracing the principles outlined in the new laws, libraries in India can transform into vibrant information centers that effectively serve their communities in the digital era. These laws provide guidance and direction for libraries to adapt, innovate, and remain relevant in an ever-changing technological and societal landscape. As libraries in India navigate the digital frontier, they have the opportunity to connect people, promote learning, foster innovation, and build strong communities that thrive in the digital age.

Courses should emphasize digital literacy education, teaching students how to critically evaluate online sources, navigate digital resources, and use technology responsibly. Privacy education should be integrated, covering data protection laws, user data management, and ethical considerations in the digital realm.Courses should include modules dedicated to understanding the new laws of library science, such as data protection regulations, copyright laws, and intellectual freedom principles. Ethical considerations related to technology, data privacy, and information access should be woven throughout the curriculum.

Practical training in using library management systems, digital catalogs, and online resources should be a core component of the curriculum.Students should gain experience in implementing technologies that enhance user experiences and compliance with new laws.Curriculum updates should reflect the shift towards digital content management, covering topics like e-books, digital archives, and online databases.Students should learn how to acquire, organize, and provide access to digital resources while adhering to copyright laws.

Courses should explore innovative ways libraries can engage with diverse communities, including virtual programming, partnerships, and inclusive services.Inclusivity training should cover accessible design, serving marginalized communities, and addressing social disparities.Courses should teach students how to manage user data, ensuring compliance with data protection regulations and maintaining user privacy.Training on cybersecurity best practices should be integrated to protect library systems and user information.

Curriculum should emphasize collaboration with IT professionals, legal experts, and community stakeholders to implement and uphold new laws effectively.Students should develop interdisciplinary skills to foster innovation and collaboration within the library ecosystem.Courses should equip students with skills to assess the impact of library programs and services in alignment with the new laws.Data analytics training can help students measure outcomes and make data-driven decisions.Courses should explore the societal impact of technology, including issues like algorithmic bias, digital divide, and digital inclusion.

Students should be prepared to address these challenges in their roles as information professionals.Curriculum updates should address ethical challenges related to information access, privacy, and intellectual freedom in the context of evolving technologies.Students should develop a strong understanding of their professional responsibilities in the digital age.Updating library science courses to align with new laws involves a holistic approach that prepares students to navigate the changing landscape of information access, digital services, and user privacy while upholding ethical and legal standards.

References

1. Babu, B. Ramesh. "Relevance of five laws of library science in the contemporary library world." *Journal of the Korean Society for Library and Information Science* 45.4 (2011): 253-269.
2. Chandratre, Shripad V., and Meghana S. Chandratre. "Marketing of library and information services."

Journal of Commerce and Management Thought 6.1 (2015): 162-175.

3. Chowdhury, Gobinda G., and Sudatta Chowdhury. Introduction to digital libraries. Facet publishing, 2003.
4. Gul, Sumeer, and Shohar Bano. "Smart libraries: an emerging and innovative technological habitat of 21st century." The Electronic Library (2019).
5. Gupta, Dinesh K. "Marketing of library and information services: building a new discipline for library and information science education in Asia." Malaysian Journal of Library & Information Science 8.2 (2003): 95-108.
6. Kumar, S. K., B. Ramesh Babu, and P. Nageswara Rao. "Implications of Five Laws of Library Science on Dr. SR Ranganathan's Colon Classification: An Explorative Study." Journal of the Korean Society for Library and Information Science 45.4 (2011): 309-326.
7. Leiter, Richard A. "Reflections on Ranganathan's five laws of library science." Law Libr. J. 95 (2003): 411.
8. Ranganathan, Shiyali Ramamrita. The five laws of library science. Madras Library Association (Madras, India) and Edward Goldston (London, UK), 1931.
9. Rubin, Richard E. Foundations of library and information science. American Library Association, 2017.
10. Weiner, Sharon Gray. "Resistance to change in libraries: Application of communication theories." portal: Libraries and the Academy 3.1 (2003): 69-78.